THEREFORE AND WHEREFORE

In the Writings of Apostle Paul

2019

Jim Webb

INTRODUCTION

THEREFORE: an adverb, which means "as a result" or implies a "consequence," or "for that reason." It is used to introduce a conclusion that follows based on logical thought. It is used in thirteen of the fourteen epistles of Paul, a total of 119 times.

WHEREFORE: an adverb, which means "why" or "for what reason" or "therefore." It is used in thirteen of the fourteen epistles of Paul, a total of 57 times.

    It is no secret that Paul teaches the doctrines and practices of the church in his epistles in a very orderly and logical manner. Throughout his writings, he establishes a fact or doctrine or truth, and then uses it to show or reach a certain conclusion or result. It is reasonable to assume that the doctrines and practices of the church are orderly and logical to those wishing to be obedient to Bible teaching.

    The purpose of this writing is to point out, within the theme of each of Paul's books, the facts or doctrines referred to and the conclusion or action that is pointed out in the logic used by the words therefore and wherefore.

TABLE OF CONTENTS

1	Title Page
2	Introduction
3	Table of Contents
4	Romans
21	I Corinthians
35	II Corinthians
46	Galatians
51	Ephesians
58	Philippians
62	Colossians
65	I Thessalonians
69	II Thessalonians
70	I Timothy
73	II Timothy

76   Titus

77   Philemon

79   Hebrews

93   Conclusion

ROMANS: The fact that Paul wrote this epistle before he had visited Rome was a good reason for him to lay a foundation of truth for them which became a foundation for all the other epistles. It was not his first epistle written but was placed first in the Bible order because of its foundational principles. **The theme of the book of Romans is "justification by faith."** Like the book of Genesis, it shows the failure of man but the deliverance of God. Note the passive tense in chapter 5, "Therefore being justified by faith, we have peace with God through our Lord Jesus Christ:" The subject of salvation is totally accomplished by what God has done. A famous list of those things God has done is in chapter 8. True church doctrine leads to obedient and thankful church practice, and the teaching of that especially begins in chapter 12. The doctrine of the church must begin with what God has done and with his purposes and promises. The practice of

the church must be the worship that results from harmony with the actions, leading, and blessings of God. The outlook and guide to God's people in the Old Testament had been the law, given to Moses at Sinai. The outlook and guide of God's people in the New Testament is now through the church, which is through Christ who has accomplished the fulfillment of the law and the release of his people from its bondage. "For the law of the Spirit of life in Christ Jesus hath made me free from the law of sin and death." (Romans 8:2)

(Romans 1:24) "**Wherefore** God also gave them up to uncleanness through the lusts of their own hearts, to dishonor their own bodies between themselves:" The theme is "justification by faith" and the first chapter of Romans begins by describing why Gentiles need justification. Paul has just listed many reasons. They didn't know God, they were not thankful, they were vain and foolish while professing themselves to be wise, they made images and idols of corruptible things to worship. All these are the "wherefore." The conclusion from these is that by nature they are polluted, wicked, and full of an unclean, dishonorable, and scandalous nature. With this nature they would never be able to stand justified before God.

(Romans 2:1) "**Therefore** thou art inexcusable, O man, whosoever thou art that judgest: for wherein thou judgest another, thou condemnest thyself; for thou that judgest doest the same things." The second chapter of Romans continues by showing why the Jews also needed justification. After listing those attributes of the natural man shown by Gentiles, it is pointed out that the Jews were judging and condemning the Gentiles for this nature when they had the same nature themselves. "Therefore" points to the Jews not being better than the Gentiles by nature, but to the conclusion that it is inexcusable that they judge the Gentiles guilty when they were guilty of the very same nature.

(Romans 2:21) "Thou **therefore** which teachest another, teachest thou not thyself? Thou that preaches a man should not steal, dost thou steal?" The second chapter of Romans describes why the Jews are also in need of justification. The Gentiles did not have the law, so did not obey the law. The Jews were given the law, but they also were not able to obey it even though they taught it from start to finish. The "therefore" is showing that even though the law was given to them, they had not kept it. The conclusion was that they are just as guilty of breaking it as the Gentiles.

(Romans 2:26) "**Therefore** if the uncircumcision keep the righteousness of the law, shall not his uncircumcision be counted for circumcision?" This second chapter of Romans is telling the need which the Jews also have for justification. "Therefore" is pointing to the fact that they were given the law and the identity of being God's people by the mark of circumcision. But the conclusion is that circumcision did not justify them and did not make them righteous before God.

(Romans 3:20) "**Therefore** by the deeds of the law there shall no flesh be justified in his sight: for by the law is the knowledge of sin." The third chapter of Romans is showing that the Jew and the Gentile are equal in their need for justification. What advantage then hath the Jew? They were given the oracles of God, but does that make them better than the Gentiles? The fact stated before the "therefore" is that there is none righteous, no not one, and that all are under sin and have come short of the glory of God. And the conclusion is that by the deeds of the law no man is justified before God because the law only points out the nature and sin of all men and convicts them guilty.

(Romans 3:28) "**Therefore** we conclude that a man is justified by faith without the deeds of the law." The third chapter points out God's view of all men under the law. Because of his nature and sin, no man can stand justified before God by keeping the law because no man can keep the law. The "therefore" here is self-explanatory as it concludes in the very words of the verse, that a man is justified by faith without the deeds of the law.

(Romans 4:16) "**Therefore** it is of faith, that it might be by grace; to the end of the promise might be sure to all the seed; not to that only which is of the law, but to that also which is of the faith of Abraham; who is the father of us all," The message of chapter four is the description of faith and grace, starting with Abraham as an example. The promise given to Abraham was not the result of the law but of God who was the source of his faith. The result was that Abraham became known as the "father of the faithful." To be justified before God requires a gift that God himself has given - faith.

(Romans 4:22) "And **therefore** it was imputed to him for righteousness." Chapter four gives the example of Abraham, who by faith believed the promise of God, in leaving his home and following God's leading, of having a son at an advanced age, and giving all the glory to God. The result, the "therefore" was that his faith was imputed to (credited for) righteousness. And he is an example for believers in Christ, and it is imputed to us also for the faith in the one who was raised up from the dead, who was delivered for our offenses, and was raised again for our justification.

(Romans 5:1) "**Therefore** being justified by faith, we have peace with God through our Lord Jesus Christ:" Chapter five is about the blessings of those who are justified by those things which accompany it. Chapter four has just described how we are justified by faith in the work of Christ which justifies us. The result of this is the conclusion reached by the "therefore" in this verse which begins chapter five. Justification causes a peace with God, and not only that but access to grace, the rejoicing of hope, the work of patience, and the understanding that Christ did this for sinners when they were still ungodly.

(Romans 5:12) "**Wherefore**, as by one man sin entered into the world, and death by sin; and so death passed upon all men, for that all have sinned:" Chapter five highlights the blessings that come by justification. The "wherefore" refers to how men are reconciled to God by the death of his son which accomplished the atonement. The comparison of "wherefore" is that sin and death had entered the world by one man, Adam; and that the gift of righteousness shall reign in eternal life by one man, Jesus.

(Romans 5:18) "**Therefore** as by the offence of one, judgment came upon all men to condemnation; even so by the righteousness of one the free gift came upon all men unto justification of life." Chapter five shows the blessings that accompany justification. The fact that this "therefore" depends on is the conclusion given for verse twelve. The result and conclusion are that one man brought condemnations by his offence, and one man brought justification by his righteousness. This sin which had brought death to all men, is now defeated by the righteousness of Christ which brings eternal life (the opposite of death).

(Romans 6:4) "**Therefore** we are buried with him by baptism into death: that like as Christ was raised up from the dead by the glory of the Father, even so we also should walk in newness of life." Chapter six shows the meaning of baptism to the Christian. What is referred to by the "therefore" is the death of Christ which accomplished the atonement. Baptism signifies the death of Christ. But the result or conclusion is that Christ was raised up from that death. And our baptism is the symbol of our new life, being raised up from the death to sin.

(Romans 6:12) "Let not sin **therefore** reign in your mortal body, that ye should obey it in the lusts thereof." The lesson of chapter six is the comparison of the meaning of baptism to the life of God's child. The fact pointed to is that one who is justified by faith and being raised in baptism as Christ was raised from the dead, should live in a way that death under the law no longer had dominion over him. The conclusion of the "therefore" is that we are no longer under the law, but now under grace and our lives should be ruled by it.

(Romans 7:4) "**Wherefore,** my brethren, ye also are become dead to the law by the body of Christ; that ye should be married to another, even to him who is raised from the dead, that we should bring forth fruit unto God." The lessons of chapter seven are concerning the struggle of a sinner to please God. The fact of "wherefore" is given in the example of marriage. The binding of it lasts until death, but when death comes then the bond and attachment of marriage is broken. When man has died to the law, its binding power over him is broken. The conclusion is that he is freed from it and serves not the oldness of the letter of the law but in newness of the spirit.

(Romans 7:12) "**Wherefore** the law is holy, and the commandment holy, and just, and good." The lesson of chapter seven is the struggle of a sinner to please God. Even though man has received this gift of grace, he is still a sinner and much conflict occurs between his nature and grace. The result is that one often does what he would not and doesn't do what he would. The soul seems to be a captive to his nature. The flesh and spirit are often warring against each other. Then he is led to the question of how can he be delivered from this body of death? The flesh serves the law of sin, but the soul serves the law of God.

(Romans 8:1) "There is **therefore** now no condemnation to them which are in Christ Jesus, who walk not after the flesh, but after the Spirit." The lesson of chapter eight is about the effectiveness and result of the works of God. In chapter seven, man has asked how he can be delivered from this body of death. The law condemns and declares it guilty. But the "therefore" in this verse shows the result that there is no condemnation to those which are in Christ Jesus, who walk not after the flesh, but after the

Spirit. The work of Christ has paid the dept and fulfilled the law for those who were guilty. The condemnation is taken away.

(Romans 8:12) "**Therefore**, brethren, we are debtors, not to the flesh, to live after the flesh," The lessons of chapter eight are about the works of God. When man was under the law, he was under death; but now under grace, he is quickened to life. "Therefore" here means that we are under a debt to the one who caused this condition. This chapter goes on to describe it and tells who are the sons of God. Even though sinful men have tribulation, these are not equal in comparison to the glory that shall be revealed. Man may sin and err, but God does not. All his works work together for good. The list of his works is given here, and it is confirmed that nothing can separate God's people from his love.

(Romans 9:18) "**Therefore** hath he mercy on whom he will have mercy, and whom he will he hardeneth." The lesson of chapter nine is that God has the power to carry out his divine purposes and promises. "Therefore" is referring to the fact that it is not by the works that men have done but is solely by the election and purposes of God that salvation has been bestowed. Therefore, God has the right and power to bestow blessings, mercy, or punishment on whoever he chooses and however he chooses to do it. He is the potter and men are the clay.

(Romans 9:32) "**Wherefore**? Because they sought it not by faith, but as it were by the works of the law. For they stumbled at that stumblingstone;" The lesson of chapter nine is concerning the purposes and promises of God. The "wherefore" is once more comparing the condition between the Gentiles and the Jews. The Jews were given the law but were not able to fulfill it. Why? Because they sought to fulfill it by works rather than by faith. It caused them to stumble and fail. Christ became a stumblingstone for all who live under the law, because justification is by faith in him, not in works of the law.

(Romans 11:22) "Behold **therefore** the goodness and severity of God: on them which fell, severity; but toward thee, goodness, if thou continue in his goodness: otherwise thou also shalt be cut off." The lesson in chapter eleven concerns the difference between national Israel and spiritual Israel. By faith the Gentile believers have been grafted in to be part of spiritual Israel. Preceding this verse is a description of the pruning and grafting in. Following it is a description of the wisdom and goodness of God to accomplish these things, "the depth of the riches both of the wisdom and knowledge of God! How unsearchable are his judgments and his ways past finding out!"

(Romans 12:1) "I beseech you **therefore**, brethren, by the mercies of God, that ye present your bodies a living sacrifice, holy, acceptable unto God, which is your reasonable service." The lesson of chapter twelve is considering what God has done, what should his people be like? Pointing back at the facts, God's children owe him a great debt. The law demanded sacrifices, and grace also demands them, but for a different reason. God's people should show their thanksgiving in ways that praise and glorify God for what he has done. Rather than giving up something of value like a bull or a lamb, a man should live his entire life in a way that uses the gifts and grace that accompany justification. To use the gifts that God has given for good will be a living sacrifice that is acceptable.

(Romans 12:20) "**Therefore** if thine enemy hunger, feed him; if he thirst give him drink: for in so doing thou shalt heap coals of fire on his head." The lesson of chapter twelve is considering what God has done, what should his people be like? Just as life and death are opposite, the behavior of a justified man and one who is not is opposite. The behavior of one is based on natural man, the behavior of the other is based on spiritual man. The law may have said an eye for an eye. But grace says turn the other cheek. Good and evil are enemies. The natural way to fight evil is with evil. The spiritual way is to overcome evil with good.

(Romans 13:2) "Whosoever **therefore** resisteth the power, resisteth the ordinance of God: and they that resist shall receive to themselves damnation." The thirteenth chapter is about submission to God. The previous verse tells that the soul is subject to higher powers, and God, and that what he has ordained is the only power. And the conclusion of that is that there is a punishment to those who resist God's power.

(Romans 13:5) "**Wherefore** ye must needs be subject, not only for wrath, but also for conscience sake." The thirteenth chapter is about submission to God. The previous verses refer to the fact of the danger and punishment of those who resist God's power and truth. The conclusion however, is that men should not only consider God's wrath and power to act upon it, but their own conscience to do what is good and right.

(Romans 13:7) "Render **therefore** to all their dues: tribute to whom tribute is due; custom to whom custom; fear to whom fear; honour to whom honour." The lesson of chapter thirteen is about submission to God. The children of God have a duty and responsibility to use spiritual judgement in life and in church matters and acceptable behavior toward others under all circumstances. It is not wise to rebel against the order of things or people which God has set in place. In concluding this thought, the ten commandments are referred to. God gave those and they are just and right. They are not the basis for salvation, but they are moral standards established by God himself.

(Romans 13:10) "Love worketh no ill to his neighbor**:** **therefore** love is the fulfilling of the law." The lesson of chapter thirteen is the submission and service to God. In the previous two verses, the commandments are referred to, and especially the treatment of other people. This verse is referring to loving thy neighbor as thyself. The conclusion of the thought is telling the practical result of abiding by God's instruction. Love will not harm one's neighbors.

(Romans 13:12) "The night is far spent, the day is at hand: let us **therefore** cast off the works of darkness, and let us put on the armour of light." The lesson of the thirteenth chapter is the submission and service to God. The time when a man was not aware of justification and grace are referred to as darkness and night. But now that a child of God understands, he is blessed with the understanding and light of day. It is time to throw off the "works" of darkness and prepare for the works of those who are justified and under the guidance of grace. The "therefore" is to put away the things of the flesh and take on the things of the spirit of Christ.

(Romans 14:8) "For whether we live, we live unto the Lord; and whether we die, we die unto the Lord: whether we live **therefore**, or die, we are the Lord's." The lesson of chapter fourteen is concerning the exercise of spiritual judgement by those who are justified. The first verses of this chapter point out the differences between people and their perceptions of each other. These differences require judgement but also an understanding that it is better to look at things as through God's eyes, seeing those who are justified, than through men's eyes and let the natural man cause conflict. It is a sure thing that God will judge his people because they are his.

(Romans 14:13) "Let us not **therefore** judge one another any more: but judge this rather, that no man put a stumblingblock or an occasion to fall in his brother's way." The lesson of chapter fourteen is the exercise of spiritual judgement. The result of judging someone else usually ends up with punishment or revenge or some other negative behavior by the one who judges. The previous verse tells the importance of judging is to give account of "himself" to God. This is a scriptural way of saying "mind your own business" not your neighbor's. It is certainly wrong to intentionally try to set someone up to fail or caught or shamed.

(Romans 14:19) "Let us **therefore** follow after the things which make for peace, and things wherewith one may edify another." The lesson of chapter fourteen is the exercise of spiritual judgement. Examples are given here, using the terms "meat and drink" which are referring to what someone uses or does. Instead of quarreling over those, it says the kingdom of God is "righteousness and peace" so men are to look for ways to build up and edify each other rather than ways to disagree or be offended. It is a worthy sacrifice to do without those things which might offend a brother. Someone with faith should have enough strength to do this and be happy that such a sacrifice would cause peace.

(Romans 15:7) "**Wherefore** receive ye one another, as Christ also received us to the glory of

God." The lesson of chapter fifteen is that Jesus is the example for Christians. This chapter begins by telling that the strong should bear the infirmities of the weak and not to please ourselves. This is a good description of Christ. Then it tells how the scriptures have been given so that the believer might have patience, comfort, and hope and exhorts the reader to be likeminded toward each other like Christ. The following verses remind again of the calling of the Gentiles and of justification being by faith in Christ, not works or circumcision.

(Romans 15:17) "I have **therefore** whereof I may glory through Jesus Christ in those things which pertain to God." The lesson of chapter fifteen is that Jesus is the example for all Christians. The verse prior reminds that it is Paul's own calling to be the minister unto the Gentiles and that they are sanctified by the same Spirit which called him, and that his ministry and teaching are sent by the same Spirit. It continues to name Christ as the example and guide that he follows in teaching the Gentiles. Those things he is teaching, he has learned from Christ.

(Romans 15:28) "When **therefore** I have performed this, and have sealed to them this fruit, I will come by you into Spain." The lesson of chapter fifteen is that Jesus is the example for all Christians. In the verses prior to this one, Paul tells his plans to visit Spain and Jerusalem and tells of the Gentile churches in Macedonia and Achaia which have sent gifts to Jerusalem. He tells that if the Gentiles have been made partakers in the spiritual things, that they should also minister to others in carnal things.

(Romans 16:19) "For your obedience is come abroad unto all men. I am glad **therefore** on your behalf: but yet I would have you wise unto that which is good, and simple concerning evil." The lesson of chapter sixteen is his commendation and warnings about who can and cannot be trusted. He points out many who have done good and some who have been a problem, causing divisions and offenses. He is thankful for the Lord's blessings to the saints at Rome and their obedience to faithfulness.

I CORINTHIANS:

Having established the foundation and doctrines of salvation for the church in the epistle to the Romans, this book is properly placed next. It sets forth the acceptable and necessary practices and spiritual judgement which must be exercised for those who are saved to continue to live and worship together in God's church. **The theme of the book of 1ˢᵗ Corinthians is spiritual judgement.** In spite of salvation, God's people are still sinners with a human nature which can destroy a spiritual church. A list of problems and instruction of correction is given in this epistle. Correct worship will lead in a path of following Christ rather than doing or allowing what human nature might lead to. Because of our nature there are two very important chapters which are vital in church worship and practice. One is chapter 13, the chapter on the importance of charity. It is a way that allows people to get along with each other in a loving way. The second is chapter 15, the chapter which is a defense of the resurrection. The church should be focused on God's power rather than the ability of man. God's promises and our hope of heaven will cause a more acceptable and profitable frame of mind for our worship and praise (the practice of the church).

(I Corinthians 3:21) "**Therefore** let no man glory in men, for all things are yours;" The subject of chapter three is that the correct understanding of the Word of God directs correct worship service and attitude. There have been envyings, strife and divisions in the church at Corinth. Those who have taught them were not divided but one laid a foundation and another built upon it. The only foundation of the church is Christ and it is not divided according to who laid its parts. There is no basis for men to think they are wiser than others. The wisdom of this world is all foolishness with God. The conclusion is that they are not to glory in who preached to them for in the scriptures they have the things of God, not the things of man. They are just like Paul, Apollos, and Cephas in that they all belong to Christ, and Christ belongs to God.

(I Corinthians 4:5) "**Therefore** judge nothing before the time, until the Lord come, who both will bring to light the hidden things of darkness, and will make manifest the counsels of the hearts: and then shall every man have praise of God." The lesson of chapter four is that Christ's ministers are stewards of Christian conduct and teaching in the church. Paul and Apollos had filled the place of stewards of the church and are not judged by how much they know but how faithful they are. It is going to be this way until the Lord comes again.

(I Corinthians 4:16) "**Wherefore** I beseech you, be ye followers of me." The lesson of chapter four is that Christ's ministers are stewards of

Christian conduct in the church. In the previous verses, the conditions and tribulations of the ministry and apostles is described as a warning, that Paul has been sent to them and not to look further for lots of other ministers. He has established them in the truth. The conclusion is that they are to follow him who was willing to go through these hardships for their sake.

(I Corinthians 5:7) "Purge out **therefore** the old leaven, that ye may be a new lump, as ye are unleavened. For even Christ our Passover is sacrificed for us:" The lesson of chapter five concerns impurity and immorality. The report that Paul had heard was that there was sexual immorality among them, and they are instructed to purge out the leaven (immorality) from the bread (the church) before it spread and corrupted everyone and everything.

(I Corinthians 5:8) "**Therefore** let us keep the feast, not with old leaven, neither with the leaven of malice and wickedness; but with the unleavened bread of sincerity and truth." The lesson of chapter five concerns impurity and immorality. In the previous verse Paul has given the example of leaven that must be purged, or it will corrupt everyone. In this verse he applies it to the unleavened bread of the communion supper, a symbol of their worship, telling that all their worship could become corrupted.

(I Corinthians 5:13) "But them that are without God judgeth. **Therefore** put away from among yourselves that wicked person." The lesson of chapter five concerns impurity and immorality. The previous verses condemn those who are a fornicator, or covetous, or an idolater, or a railer, or a drunkard, or an extortioner, and instructs the church at Corinth to separate them from the church and not eat with them (commune).

(I Corinthians 6:7) "Now **therefore** there is utterly a fault among you, because ye go to law one with another. Why do ye not rather take wrong? Why do ye not rather suffer yourselves to be defrauded?" The lesson of chapter six concerns lawsuits among the members. The previous verses have pointed out that it is shameful for members of the church to take issues to those outside the church to be publicly solved. In further instruction it is pointed out the importance of what is wise and expedient over what is lawful. Paul further points out that our body is not our own but the temple of the Holy Ghost and that ye are bought with a price.

(I Corinthians 7:8) "I say **therefore** to the unmarried and widows, It is good for them if they abide even as I." The lessons of chapter seven are concerning marriage. Paul describes what marriage should be, but in this verse also says it is acceptable for someone to remain unmarried like himself. But faithfulness is required of whichever state is chosen.

(I Corinthians 7:26) "I suppose **therefore** that this is good for the present distress, I say, that it is good for a man so to be." The lessons of chapter seven are concerning marriage. In the previous verses Paul has described different conditions of marriage or celibacy. He points out the responsibility and acceptable possibilities of each circumstance.

(I Corinthians 8:4) "As concerning **therefore** the eating of those things that are offered in sacrifice unto idols, we know that an idol is nothing in the world, and that there is none other God but one." The lessons of chapter eight are about Christian liberty. The issue here is whether it is acceptable to eat things which have been offered to idols. He points out that there are many gods, lords, and idols, but only one God. He says that men are not better off for avoiding or worse off for doing, but that one should be careful in taking this liberty, to not be a stumbling block to them that are weak or disagree.

(I Corinthians 8:13) "**Wherefore**, if meat make my brother to offend, I will eat no flesh while the world standeth, lest I make my brother to offend." The subject of the lessons of chapter eight concern Christian liberty. The Christian has been freed from making sacrifices of animals to God because of the perfect sacrifice of Christ. But can he partake of things that have been sacrificed to idols and heathen gods? Is it a blasphemy toward God to do this? While Paul does not say that it is wrong, he does say that he would not do it if it offended a brother. The relationship of brethren is more important than some practice that is based on carnal hunger.

(I Corinthians 9:26) "I **therefore** so run, not as uncertainly; so fight I, not as one that beateth the air:" The subject of chapter nine is Christian liberty. Paul begins this chapter with a question, "am I not free?" It is in this chapter that he points out that he does not do this work of the ministry for money. He is free from the obligation to preach a certain way for them because they do not provide his living. He answers to God, but asks the Corinthians what is his prize. Then in the verses before this one, he describes running a race to receive a prize. He has not run for no reason and his position is secure because he has run (ministered to them) with the truth, so that when he is finished, he will not become a castaway having accomplished nothing.

(I Corinthians 10:12) "**Wherefore** let him that thinketh he standeth take heed lest he fall." The subject in chapter ten is concerning temptations to the people of God. The chapter begins by telling how God has kept his people through the ages, but the importance of their being disciplined, and not think that just because they are God's they can do anything and get away with it. God's blessings are tied to the obedience to his admonitions. The one who is over-confident in his own self but undisciplined in behavior is ready for a hard fall.

(I Corinthians 10:14) "**Wherefore**, my dearly beloved, flee from idolatry." The subject of chapter ten is lessons concerning temptations. Paul describes that God will not allow temptations that are not common to all people, or that are impossible to bear, or which have no way of escape, but the warning for some temptations is that the way to escape them is to flee from them.

(I Corinthians 10:31) "Whether **therefore** ye eat, or drink, or whatsoever ye do, do all to the glory of God." The subject of chapter ten is dealing with temptations. In avoiding idolatry, once again the subject arises of eating what has been offered to idols. This time another case is mentioned, that some Gentiles make offerings to devils, and they are not to eat of those. An idol is a nothing, but a devil is a devil. There will be times where the decision is based on whether it offends someone, and then refrain. The general answer to what is done should be this verse, to do whatever one does to the glory of God. A person should not do what would offend God.

(I Corinthians 11:20) "When ye come together **therefore** into one place, this is not to eat the Lord's supper." The subject of the first part of chapter eleven is about women in the church and of the second part a discussion and correction of their observance of the Lord's supper. The verses before this show that there were divisions among them and possible heresies present. Before entering into this solemn service, it is necessary that these things be settled and that the communion be observed properly as it was intended and with the meanings of it followed correctly. It is not a normal meal and its observance is not to be taken lightly.

(I Corinthians 11:27) "**Wherefore** whosoever shall eat this bread, and drink this cup of the Lord, unworthily, shall be guilty of the body and blood of the Lord." The subject of the last half of chapter eleven is the observance of the Lord's supper. Paul has just given a description of the Lord's supper and its meaning and seriousness. The "wherefore" here doubles down on the warning of taking part in this in an unworthy manner. It is not an offense to men, but to Christ, who gave his life.

(I Corinthians 11:33) "**Wherefore**, my brethren, when ye come together to eat, tarry one for another." The subject is the observance of the Lord's supper. In the previous verses, Paul has stated that because the Lord's supper has been improperly observed there are many who are weak and unaware of its seriousness and meaning. So there is a duty that the participants should wait on each other and share together the things that would make it correct and meaningful and understood.

(I Corinthians 12:3) "**Wherefore** I give you to understand, that no man speaking by the Spirit of God calleth Jesus accursed: and that no man can say that Jesus is the Lord, but by the Holy Ghost." Chapter twelve is concerning spiritual gifts. Paul addresses them, knowing that as Gentiles they have worshipped idols and participated in curses and diverse practices which are not acceptable in the church. He sets the tone of what is to be done and how God is to be approached and spoken of by the proper spirit in the church in these first several verses of chapter twelve.

(I Corinthians 12:15-16) "If the foot shall say, Because I am not the hand, I am not of the body; is it **therefore** not of the body? And if the ear shall say, Because I am not the eye, I am not of the body; is it therefore not of the body?" The subject of chapter twelve is concerning spiritual gifts that make up the body of the church. The explanation begins that people make up many members of one body and all are necessary to work together for the good of the one body. If the foot was a hand, the body could not walk. If the ear were an eye, then the body could not hear. It is necessary for every gift to do its own work. When any part of the body suffers, then all the body suffers. And when any part is honoured, all the body rejoices together. Paul lists some of the gifts: apostles, prophets, teachers, miracles, gifts of healing, helps, governments, and diversities of tongues.

(I Corinthians 14:11) "**Therefore** if I know not the meaning of the voice, I shall be unto him that speaketh a barbarian, and he that speaketh shall be a barbarian unto me." Chapter fourteen is about gifts and the speaking of tongues. The subject of this chapter is "edification" and the gifts compared are prophecy and speaking in tongues. In the verses prior to this the word edification is used four times and it is used again in the next verse. There is no point in speaking in tongues if no one knows the meaning of what is uttered. On the other hand, the gift of prophecy is one that reveals the unknown.

I Corinthians 14:13) "**Wherefore** let him that speaketh in an unknown tongue pray that he may interpret." The subject of this verse again concerns the gifts in the church. It is told that the purpose of the gifts of God are for the edification of the church. Not being understood is not to the edification of the church. Interpreting is with the purpose of understanding and explaining the scripture. The word "edification" is used in the verse before this and again several verses later.

(I Corinthians 14:22-23) "**Wherefore** tongues are for a sign, not to them that believe, but to them that believe not: but prophesying serveth not for them that believe not, but for them which believe. If therefore the whole church be come together into one place, and all speak with tongues, and there come in those that are unlearned, or unbelievers, will they not say that ye are mad?"

Once more the subject is about gifts and the speaking in tongues. The purpose of gifts is to promote understanding. God used this gift at an appropriate time to cause a great effect and it was instrumental in the start and spread of the church. The wonder of it was that everyone understood what was being said in their own language. But if used as these two verses describe, not only will no one gain understanding from it, but it will be ridiculed.

(I Corinthians 14:39) "**Wherefore,** brethren, covet to prophesy, and forbid not to speak with tongues." A final verse is found here concerning the use of speaking with tongues. Paul's instruction is not to forbid the speaking of tongues, but to actually prefer the gift of prophecy which will be edifying to the church.

(I Corinthians 15:11) "**Therefore** whether it were I or they, so we preach, and so ye believed." Chapter fifteen is a description and defense of the resurrection. Paul had preached to them what he had witnessed and received himself. Christ had died for our sins, was buried, and rose again the third day. Then he gave a long list of those who were also witnesses, listing himself last. The doctrine of the resurrection is the truth no matter who preaches it. What follows is that Paul defends it in every possible way to those who say it cannot be so.

(I Corinthians 15:58) "**Therefore**, my beloved brethren, be ye stedfast, unmoveable, always abounding in the work of the Lord, forasmuch as ye know that your labour is not in vain in the Lord." The result of all these proofs about the truth of the resurrection is that believers now have hope and know that their labors and faithfulness are not in vain. The final enemy, death, was defeated, and the victory over it was placed on the elect, so that of all those given him, he should lose nothing, but raise them up again on the last day.

(I Corinthians 16:11) "Let no man **therefore** despise him: but conduct him forth in peace, that he may come unto me: for I look for him with the brethren." The message in this chapter is the farewell and benediction of the epistle. In the farewell, Paul tells the possibility of Timothy coming to see the church in Rome and instructs them to receive and protect him and send him on to Paul.

(I Corinthians 16:18) "For they have refreshed my spirit and yours: **therefore** acknowledge ye them that are such." Also in his farewell, Paul expresses that he is thankful for Stephanus, Fortunatus, and Achaicus who have helped him. He instructs them to encourage them and other like persons for that kind of service to the church.

II CORINTHIANS:
Correcting anyone will always cause a reaction which questions a person's authority. Sometimes it is called into question by those being corrected, and sometimes it can be a doubt created within. Paul had lived in Corinth more than a year and knew the people there and their environment well. He also knew what was right and what was wrong, and he knew what things would cause the destruction of the church. Even further, he knew what his calling was and had strong faith that God had given him that calling. **The theme of the epistle of 2nd Corinthians is Christian calling.** Everyone who stands for right is going to be challenged by those who disagree. Paul defends his right to correct and exercise spiritual judgement in the very first sentence, by these words "Paul, an apostle of Jesus Christ by the will of God." Throughout the ages, the church has continued because there were always some faithful who were willing to exercise their spiritual judgement and defend their calling

on behalf of the church and its practices. The church is God's. People who live in it have an obligation to follow God's instruction. Paul was not teaching his own opinions and wishes, but what God had instituted. No true church has the right to make its own choices and decisions or say what it will accept or do, except only to obey what God has instructed. All Christians will be challenged in their calling. If God's instructions are followed, then anyone disagreeing will be disagreeing with God, not man.

(II Corinthians 1:17) "When I **therefore** was thus minded, did I use lightness? Or the things that I purpose, do I purpose according to the flesh, that with me there should be yea yea, and nay nay?" Paul had come to the church in Corinth before and had lived there for more than a year and had made plans to come to them again (in verse 15) but was unable to before this letter. He is saying here that he had not taken lightly his promise to be with them or the reasons for it. His first epistle to them had been full of correction. Rather than come and continue that in a way that they might feel he was exercising dominion over them, they are given time to work things out among themselves so that his next visit might be one of encouraging their joy and worship rather than one of correction. The result of his calling and his correcting should be the health and edification of the church.

(II Corinthians 2:8) "**Wherefore** I beseech you that ye would confirm your love toward him." The corrections of the circumstances in the first letter to the church at Corinth had weighed heavy on them. The actions required in those corrections were not complete by themselves, but also required of the church that they be done in a loving and charitable rather than a hateful or vengeful spirit. Even though tough action was required, it should not remove the fellowship or close feelings between the members.

(II Corinthians 4:1) "**Therefore** seeing we have this ministry, as we have received mercy, we faint not;" In the previous chapter, Paul has referred to how Moses put a veil over his face. That veil is symbolic of how the people were blinded to the answer of the law which Christ fulfilled. The people had already broken the first two commandments before Moses could bring them down from the mountain. They were deserving of death, but through prayer and God's purposes, the law was tempered with mercy and grace. Paul had been one who persecuted the church and believers, but when Christ was revealed, the veil was removed and he by mercy and grace saw the truth and understood Christ's ministry and then the ministry which he was directed into also… his calling.

(II Corinthians 4:13) "We having the same spirit of faith, according as it is written, I believed, and **therefore** have I spoken; we also believe, and therefore speak;" The verses preceding this are well-known. "we are troubled on every side, yet not distressed; we are perplexed, but not in despair. Persecuted, but not forsaken; cast down, but not destroyed." Obeying the call to the work a man is given will require his taking on burdens and hardships which reflect what Christ suffered in his ministry. The death of Christ had caused the life and faith of the elect. And Paul compares it to his own suffering in the ministry which brings life and faith into the church. The very next verse points out the conclusion of this verse: "Knowing that he which raised up the Lord Jesus shall raise up us also by Jesus and shall present us with you."

(II Corinthians 5:6) "**Therefore** we are always confident, knowing that, whilst we are at home in the body, we are absent from the Lord:" The subject of the fifth chapter is the comfort of God. It begins by telling that even though our earthly house is destroyed, we have a building of

God which is eternal. It is God who has created this and given us a preview of what is to come. So the conclusion is that we can be confident and as stated in the next verse, walk by faith, not by sight.

(II Corinthians 5:9) "**Wherefore** we labour, that, whether present or absent, we may be accepted of him." This verse refers to verses six and eight, where it is speaking of when being at home in our body we are absent from the Lord, and being absent from our body we are present with God. So the result, by faith, is that we labour to be acceptable to God whether we are present or absent.

(II Corinthians 5:11) "Knowing **therefore** the terror of the Lord, we persuade men; but we are made manifest unto God; and I trust also are made manifest in your consciences." The terror spoken of is from the previous verse, where it is stated that all must appear before the judgement seat of Christ. Also that everyone will receive the result of having done good or bad according to the works of their calling. God knows what we have done and so does our conscience.

(II Corinthians 5:16) "**Wherefore** henceforth know we no man after the flesh: yea, though we have known Christ after the flesh, yet now henceforth know we him no more." This wherefore is referring to how God looks at man and how men look at each other. Once a person has been born of God, he sees through new eyes. We no longer look or judge by being "after the flesh" but by the spirit. It is also true of how we see Christ. He was here as a man, but now is in heaven. So our relationship with him is not as though he is now here in the flesh, but as he is now in glory as our intercessor with God.

(II Corinthians 5:17) "**Therefore** if any man be in Christ, he is a new creature: old things are passed away; behold, all things are become new." The previous fact of the "therefore" is the sixteenth verse. We see both men and Christ in a new way. We look forward to the day when our change will come. But a day and a change has already come where spiritual life began and man was made into a new creature. By that new life, all things are seen in a new way.

(II Corinthians 6:17) "**Wherefore** come out from among them, and be ye separate, saith the Lord, and touch not the unclean thing; and I will receive you," The sixth chapter continues to instruct in ways that will comfort the believer or prevent some of the tribulations of life. Just previous to this verse, Paul has instructed that the believer be not unequally yoked to unbelievers. Then he begins to tell about some of the problems of such a union. Unbelievers are attached to false worship and idols, and believers are instructed to come away from those things. With that instruction is the promise that God will be their father and dwell in them and walk with them.

(II Corinthians 7:1) "Having **therefore** these promises, dearly beloved, let us cleanse ourselves from all filthiness of the flesh and spirit, perfecting holiness in the fear of God." The promises of the last verse of the sixth chapter are referred to here. Having received those promises, what should we do and how should we be like? Certainly we should come away from unbelievers and their worship of false gods and idols.

(II Corinthians 7:12) "**Wherefore**, though I wrote unto you, I did it not for his cause that had done the wrong, nor for his cause that suffered wrong, but that our care for you in the sight of God might appear unto you." Comfort continues to be a lesson in the seventh chapter. Paul tells how he was comforted by the coming of Titus. Paul speaks then of their reaction to his first letter. They had mourned with godly sorrow and desired to follow his instruction. Paul states that godly sorrow worketh repentance. He had corrected them not only because they were in the wrong, but because he cared for them.

(II Corinthians 7:13) "**Therefore** we were comforted in your comfort: yea, and exceedingly the more joyed we for the joy of Titus, because his spirit was refreshed by you all." When Paul learns that they had accepted his instruction with godly repentance, he is comforted too. He also tells that Titus was comforted to see this behavior and spirit.

(II Corinthians 7:16) "I rejoice **therefore** that I have confidence in you in all things." Paul is thanking them for their obedience and their treatment of Titus and expresses that their behavior has given him confidence that things are now going in the right direction.

(II Corinthians 8:7) "**Therefore**, as ye abound in every thing, in faith, and utterance, and knowledge, and in all diligence, and in your love to us, see that ye abound in this grace also." The subject here changes to concerning assistance they are sending to the church at Jerusalem. They are commended for giving, even out of their own poverty. Paul states here that it is evidence of their blessing and obedience and diligence and their love of God to give with that attitude.

(II Corinthians 8:11) "Now **therefore** perform the doing of it; that as there was a readiness to will, so there may be a performance also out of that which ye have." Paul here uses their example to give another lesson. It is that Christ was rich and became poor, that through his poverty his people might become rich. And in the explaining of the rightness of their giving, Paul refers to a scripture of the Old Testament concerning the gathering of manna. "He that had gathered much had nothing over; and he that had gathered little had no lack."

(II Corinthians 8:24) "**Wherefore** shew ye to them, and before the churches, the proof of your love, and of our boasting on your behalf." Again the lesson is about Christian giving. Paul commends them for it and tells that they justify his boasting of their generosity.

(II Corinthians 9:5) "**Therefore** I thought it necessary to exhort the brethren, that they would go before unto you, and make up beforehand your bounty, whereof ye had notice before, that the same might be ready, as a matter of bounty, and not as of covetousness." The subject continues to be Christian giving. Again he commends them, that they have planned and pledged and then given accordingly. Their donation is called a bounty (as related to the word bountiful) here, which indicates that their gift was large.

(II Corinthians 11:11) "**Wherefore**? Because I love you not? God knoweth." Paul continues his subject of Christian calling in the tenth chapter which authenticates his apostleship. Chapter eleven vindicates his apostleship. One of the statements he makes is that he did not allow the church to contribute to his ministry. He did the work he was called to do because he was called, not because someone paid him. This also meant that he could preach the truth without owing anyone favors. He had not made himself an apostle but was called of God.

(II Corinthians 11:15) "**Therefore** it is no great thing if his ministers also be transformed as the ministers of righteousness; whose end shall be according to their works." Here Paul has referred to the fact that Satan has ministers. Just as Satan is described as an angel of light, his ministers are those who are attractive to men. But their methods and motives are selfish and self-serving. Many do it for the power and influence and to become rich.

(II Corinthians 12:9) "And he said unto me, My grace is sufficient for thee: for my strength is made perfect in weakness. Most gladly **therefore** will I rather glory in my infirmities, that the power of Christ may rest upon me." In this chapter Paul tells about being caught up into the third heaven and then about having a thorn in the flesh. The letter does not tell what the thorn was, but that God's answer to his prayer was that he would be given grace to bear it. Then it becomes an honor to have an affliction, if by it God applies his power and grace to one's circumstances.

(II Corinthians 12:10) "**Therefore** I take pleasure in infirmities, in reproaches, in necessities, in persecutions, in distresses for Christ's sake: for when I am weak, then am I strong." The conclusion of verse nine is the statement of verse ten. A man is able to bear all manner of problems if God gives him the grace to do it. Men are not worthy because of their own power, but because they are enabled by the power of God. The admission of weakness and need is the prayer that opens the door to God's power.

(II Corinthians 13:10) "**Therefore** I write these things being absent, lest being present I should use sharpness, according to the power which the Lord hath given me to edification, and not to destruction." In chapter thirteen, Paul repeats that he is coming, and once more will give the church evidence of his calling. He again mentions that a letter might seem easier than his personal critique if he were present in person. He exhorts them to examine themselves. It is easy to criticize someone else, but all men should examine if they are doing what God called them to do. He prays for them and for their strength and that his admonitions will work to their edification rather than their downfall. He concludes with final advice to them of unity and peace and that the God of love and peace be with them.

GALATIANS:
Paul was called to be an apostle to the Gentiles. In the first generation of the church, most of the Christians were Jews. Because the Jews and Gentiles were antagonists, the Jews began to believe and practice that in order to become a Christian, a person first had to become a Jew. This epistle was sent to correct the belief that Christians (either Jew or Gentile) were still bound to Jewish customs, ceremony and law. Christ had freed them from that bondage. Paul does not hesitate to tell them without other preliminary remarks that they are wrong. The best-known verse of this epistle is chapter 5:1, "Stand fast therefore in the liberty wherewith Christ hath made us free, and be not entangled again with the

yoke of bondage." **The theme of the book of Galatians is Christian liberty.**

(Galatians 2:17) "But if, while we seek to be justified by Christ, we ourselves also are found sinners, is **therefore** Christ the minister of sin? God forbid." In his opening remarks to the church at Galatia, Paul has immediately pointed out the error of their ways. He immediately lays again the foundation of salvation as it is told in the Roman letter. Justification is not by the law or by the traditions of religion or legalism. Christ has freed them from these things. The previous verse has just stated that man is not justified by works of the law but by faith in Jesus Christ and that by works of the law shall no flesh be justified. And in the verse before that he had named Gentiles as sinners by nature. The Jew must now forsake the law and become as a Gentile (sinner) in order to be justified. So the question he asks is if Christ them makes men sinners in the process of justifying them. Of course he does not. The law is what condemns men to death as sinners. Christ through faith has brought life through his justification.

(Galatians 3:5) "He **therefore** that ministereth to you the Spirit, and worketh miracles among you, doeth he it by the works of the law, or by the hearing of faith?" The third chapter continues in the subject of justification by faith. Paul begins by declaring the church of Galatia has been bewitched and asks how they had received the Spirit… by the law or by faith? If by faith, then why would they return back to the law? The question of this verse is asking them by which means that he himself had come teaching and ministering to them… by the law or faith? The answer is obvious that it is by the hearing of faith.

(Galatians 3:7) "Know ye **therefore** that they which are of faith, the same are the children of Abraham." Next Paul uses the illustration of Abraham and his faith, and Abraham was the father of the Jews. Abraham showed his faith and received the promise even before the law was given. The Gentiles were in the same position as Abraham, without the law, but justified by faith. They were not the children of Abraham by nature, but they are by the spirit. They are not children of Abraham by the law, but they are by faith.

(Galatians 3:19) "**Wherefore** then serveth the law? It was added because of transgressions, till the seed should come to whom the promise was made; and it was ordained by angels in the hand of a mediator." In the verses before this one, Paul points out that the promise about the "seed" of Abraham was given before the law. The law was added because of sin, but it did not nullify the promise. It was just temporary until the arrival of the "seed." That seed was Christ. The word is not "seeds." God was not talking about all the descendants of Abraham but of one "seed" which would be the messiah. Worship should not be for something temporary, but for the promise of God which would be forever.

(Galatians 3:24) "**Wherefore** the law was our schoolmaster to bring us unto Christ, that we might be justified by faith." Here Paul uses another illustration. He has called the law a schoolmaster. There is a purpose to a schoolmaster and that is to teach. Under the law, man learns that he is a sinner and condemned by God. However, when faith arrives, the man is released from the schoolmaster because Christ has born the guilt and paid the price and freed him from the verdict of the law. There are many benefits of faith which are not possible by the law, and those are pointed out in the next verses.

(Galatians 4:7) "**Wherefore** thou art no more a servant, but a son; and if a son, then an heir of God through Christ." In this chapter Paul begins with the purpose of showing two things. First, that by faith those who were under the law would be redeemed; and second, that they would receive the adoption of sons. The law didn't make anyone a son, but a servant. But Christ through the justification of faith did.

(Galatians 4:16) "Am I **therefore** become your enemy, because I tell you the truth?" During his ministry, Paul was aware of the "thorn in his flesh" that he named in the letter to Corinth. The church here had not held it against him that he had some weakness. God had given him sufficient grace. So he is saying that their weakness in turning back to the law is similar to his own thorn in the flesh, and that if they will, by faith, be strengthened by the grace of God to overcome it. Paul has not been easy on them or soft in telling the truth. He is not their enemy for doing it, but ministering them to a position and knowledge of strength.

(Galatians 5:1) "Stand fast **therefore** in the liberty wherewith Christ hath made us free, and be not entangled again with the yoke of bondage." Earlier Paul had addressed them that he was shocked how quickly they had departed from the truth. This could be looked at as "falling from grace" if they allowed their belief to backslide from faith back to the law. Not that they had lost their salvation, but that they would lose the comfort and peace of mind of it. Now Paul exhorts them to stand fast, to hold to that freedom which had been bestowed on them and not slide back to the works and guilt of the law.

(Galatians 6:10) "As we have **therefore** opportunity, let us do good unto all men, especially unto them who are of the household of faith." In this last chapter of Galatians, Paul uses an illustration of gardening, telling that whatsoever a man soweth, that he shall also reap. He continues in that line by telling that sowing in the flesh will reap corruption but sowing by the Spirit would reap everlasting life. Those who spend all their time serving the natural man will not get to enjoy the things which give reward to the spiritual man. His instruction is that a believer should not only be doing good while with other believers but should be doing good all the time to all men, and especially to other believers.

EPHESIANS:
There is a definition of peace that says it is an absence of hostility. But real peace is when there is a feeling of harmony and unity between the parties. The goals of a Christian and of a church include that there be fellowship

with God and between his people. That fellowship is not just an absence of hostility, but a feeling of harmony and unity. Then it becomes easy to work together and worship together. How can a sinner have fellowship with God? This epistle answers that question with two things. The first is by what God did. He chose them before the world was, he predestinated them to his heavenly inheritance, he adopted them, paid the purchase price for their sins, and then gave them spiritual life after they were born on this earth. Without these actions, which man had no part in, it would be impossible to have fellowship with God. God completed all the conditions. Second is the obedient labor of love and faith that the child of God should exercise with each other here on earth, giving evidence of their spiritual birth. This is how the child of God can feel fellowship with others in the church. There are levels of fellowship which are based on the faith, commitment, and difficulty of the path walked together. **The theme of the book of Ephesians is spiritual fellowship.**

(Ephesians 1:15) "**Wherefore** I also, after I heard of your faith in the Lord Jesus, and love unto all the saints," Chapter one begins immediately by telling what God has done, having "chosen us in him before the foundation of the world" and "predestinated us unto the adoption of children by Jesus Christ to himself" and telling that we have redemption through the blood of Christ. These things are for the purpose of our being to the praise of his glory. Then Paul gives thanks for the faith of the church at Ephesus and mentions them in his prayers.

Ephesians 2:11) "**Wherefore** remember, that ye being in time past Gentiles in the flesh, who are called Uncircumcision by that which is called the Circumcision in the flesh made by hands;" Chapter two begins in a similar way, telling what God has done, "you hath he quickened, who were dead in trespasses and sins;" and how the church is raised up together with Christ and made to sit together in heavenly places. Here is the basis for spiritual fellowship. Credit is given correctly, "For by grace are ye saved through faith; and that not of yourselves: it is the gift of God." The Gentiles which made up most of this church were not of the circumcised, which is the identity by the flesh, but now of the Spirit. Before this they were aliens and strangers from the promise.

(Ephesians 2:19) "Now **therefore** ye are no more strangers and foreigners, but fellow-citizens with the saints, and of the household of God;" But now those who were strangers and afar off are made nigh by the blood of Christ. The law is broken down so that both Jew and Gentile have no wall between them. Now they both have access to the Father. Now they are not strangers and foreigners, but fellow-citizens with the saints, and of the household of God. Now they stand on the same foundation as the apostles and prophets. Fellowship is established between them.

(Ephesians 3:13) "**Wherefore** I desire that ye faint not at my tribulations for you, which is your glory." Chapter three is about the mystery of Christ. How are these things possible? Not by earthly means. Since the time of the prophets, now these mysteries are unfolding because of what Christ has done when he came. And it became necessary for Paul to preach and teach about the fellowship of the mystery, which was hidden until the coming of Christ. That is why Paul has boldness and confidence. This being so important, and he being called to this work by God, he urges them not to be faint at his tribulations. It is for their sake that these things are revealed.

(Ephesians 4:1) "I **therefore,** the prisoner of the Lord, beseech you that ye walk worthy of the vocation wherewith ye are called," Having received such a mighty and beautiful heavenly calling, and a prisoner to God in demonstrating that calling, now Paul turns to the church and reminds them of their own calling. Now they are reminded that they also must carry a burden and give evidence of that fellowship of the mystery. It is not meant that we can be worthy of God's calling, but that worthy here means befitting, that our work be appropriate to our calling. Paul describes that in the next few verses, "with all lowliness and meekness, with longsuffering, forbearing one another in love; Endeavouring to keep the unity of the Spirit in the bond of peace."

(Ephesians 4:8) "**Wherefore** he saith, When he ascended up on high, he led captivity captive, and gave gifts unto men." This verse is a partial quotation from Psalms 68. But in that chapter it says that he received gifts for men. Here he gave gifts unto men. In Psalms it is telling that he has the gifts for the church ready, and when he came to earth he has distributed those gifts to the church by the Holy Spirit. These are further evidence and reason for the fellowship which should be present in the church.

(Ephesians 4:17) "This I say **therefore**, and testify in the Lord, that ye henceforth walk not as other Gentiles walk, in the vanity of their mind,"

The gifts that God gave the church are for its perfecting, for its edifying, and for its unity. In being strengthened together, the church should become a body that is not easily tossed about or deceived. Therefore, the church has reason to not walk in many separate ways, but to be joined together as a spiritual body. Several verses after this one give a description of that previous walk, divided and in darkness.

(Ephesians 4:25) "**Wherefore** putting away lying, speak every man truth with his neighbor: for we are members one of another." Based on what has just been taught about the unity and edifying, the man of God is then become a new creature, a new man. He is commanded to put off the old man and put on the new man in order to have control over his anger, his deeds, and his speech.

(Ephesians 5:1) "Be ye **therefore** followers of God, as dear children." The believer is not to strike out on his own, but is to be "led," now a follower of Christ. And he is also to be as obedient children of God. He is taught what things are evil and what things are good in the church, much like in the home. But the father is God, and the church is to become the bride of Christ.

(Ephesians 5:7) "Be not ye **therefore** partakers with them." In telling what things are evil, it follows that the believer is not to participate in those things and not to participate in things with those who do. This cannot happen without the displeasure and punishment of God.

(Ephesians 5:14) "**Wherefore** he saith, Awake thou that sleepest, and arise from the dead, and Christ shall give thee light." A comparison is made here that those who are not believers are in a darkness of not understanding. However, those who are believers have had light shone upon them. Those who are in darkness, sleep as though dead, while those in the light should be working and going about their business of living. The believer is commanded not to live in darkness as though he is asleep and unaware of the difference. He is to live wisely, using his time well.

(Ephesians 5:24) "**Therefore** as the church is subject unto Christ, so let the wives be to their own husbands in every thing." With a comparison here of the church being the bride of Christ, instruction is given for both the wife to be obedient to the husband and for the husband to give himself for the wife as Christ has for the church. Christ and the church are an example of how the believer should live.

(Ephesians 6:13) "**Wherefore** take unto you the whole armour of God, that ye may be able to withstand in the evil day, and having done all, to stand." The greatest level of fellowship is that relationship of soldiers fighting side by side for a cause and protecting each other. Chapter six tells the importance of being a good soldier. It tells of the protection and use of the spiritual armour and its defense against the enemy. All the armour is necessary, not just some of it, and by that withstanding the enemy is possible.

(Ephesians 6:14) "Stand **therefore,** having your loins girt about with truth, and having on the breastplate of righteousness;" When Paul says "stand" he means that the soldier not fall or not run away. The soldier should hold his ground firmly. The defense of the church is truth and God's word. If the enemy attack those, they attack God. If they attack those, God will be the strength to defend them. The defense of a soldier of the cross is to follow his God, wearing the armour that God has provided.

PHILIPPIANS: Paul began his second documented journey with a destination in mind, but in a dream was instead directed to go over into

Macedonia. He landed at Philippi and the church which was established there became a valuable encouragement to him. One of the things which determines how well a person can worship and praise is "attitude." This letter is written to the church at Philippi from prison, but one cannot detect that from Paul's attitude. There is a song which says that prisons would palaces prove if Jesus would dwell with me there. Christians and the early church were under heavy persecution. Paul was greatly persecuted and abused, but he spent little or no time complaining about it, because his saviour also was highly and unfairly abused and he did not complain but always had a perfect attitude. This church had sent him provisions and gifts multiple times. This epistle is filled with optimism and joy. **The theme of the epistle of Philippians is that our attitude is to be like the mind of Christ.** It is given in chapter 2:5, "Let this mind be in you, which was also in Christ Jesus." In a fairly short letter of four chapters, the word joy is used six times and the word rejoice is used ten times.

(Philippians 2:1) "If there be **therefore** any consolation in Christ, if any comfort of love, if any fellowship of the Spirit, if an bowels and mercies,"

The first chapter to the church at Philippi commended them highly for their faithfulness and told of Paul's condition. Chapter two begins to tell the pattern that the believer should follow. In both his need for comfort and his desire to praise, there is one who was perfect that is our guide. His instruction would make them stronger and unified if they did as directed, every man esteeming others better than self.

(Philippians 2:9) "**Wherefore** God also hath highly exalted him, and given him a name which is above every name:" The theme of the entire book is in verse five, that we live through all seasons with Christ as our example, to have the mind of Christ. What Christ gave up we cannot yet understand, but we do know that he took a position of no reputation and of a servant and was humble and obedient unto death. However, in doing these perfectly, God has exalted him and given a name above all others, and there is coming a day when at his name every knee shall bow and every tongue confess that he is Lord.

(Philippians 2:12) "**Wherefore**, my beloved, as ye have always obeyed, not as in my presence only, but how much more in my absence, work out your own salvation with fear and trembling." Paul is in prison and not able to guide them daily or answer their questions. However, they have in them the Holy Spirit who is a guide. By salvation here is meant their daily salvation, the solving of problems and tribulations of life. A believer has the instruction in the form of the Bible to handle those things correctly, to pray correctly, and the faith to walk as they should through all things.

(Philippians 2:23) "Him **therefore** I hope to send presently, so soon as I shall see how it will go with me." As a prisoner at Rome, Paul is not able to come to them at Philippi, but his intent is to send Timothy as soon as he knows a little more about the things that are happening.

(Philippians 2:28) "I sent him **therefore** the more carefully, that, when ye see him again, ye may rejoice, and that I may be the less sorrowful." Paul was also sending Epaphroditus to them, the minister they had sent to him. Paul commends him also and tells that he had been very sick.

(Philippians 2:29) "Receive him **therefore** in the Lord with all gladness; and hold such in reputation:" The church is to be thankful that Epaphroditus returns having recovered from a serious sickness and having seen Paul and bringing word of Paul's situation to them.

(Philippians 3:15) "Let us **therefore**, as many as be perfect, be thus minded: and if in any thing ye be otherwise minded, God shall reveal even this unto you." The tribulation that Paul was going through helped him to know the importance of what Christ had done. The verses preceding this one tell the importance of knowing Christ and the power of his resurrection and the fellowship of his suffering. Paul had been through a lot of things, but what he was doing and instructing them to do about their attitude was to forget those things which were behind and press forward toward the mark for the prize of the high calling of God in Christ Jesus. While keeping this attitude, if any are to be called to a special work, God will reveal it to them.

(Philippians 4:1) "**Therefore**, my brethren dearly beloved and longed for, my joy and crown, so stand fast in the Lord, my dearly beloved." Paul had a reason to love these people at this church. Their faithfulness was a great joy to him. They made him rejoice in spite of all the things he had gone through. Does this remind you of someone else? Of how Christ, for the joy that was set before him, endured the cross, despising the shame.

COLOSSIANS: This is another epistle written from prison. In this instance, a minister that he has ordained comes to visit him in prison with word that the church at Colosse is being troubled by false teaching. Before giving instruction concerning the problem, he compliments them on their faith, love, and hope. A problem comes into the church when something other than Christ's teaching comes in and seems believable. Perhaps some are saying all you believe is true, however, it is because of this and this. And then they name things that are misleading or irrelevant. Such a strategy has happened in today's church with the teaching of evolution. There is no scientific proof, but it is taught in all the schools. The facts of the Bible are explained away by something that would weaken the faith of believers. Christians and churches are to beware of the philosophies of the world. **The theme of the book of Colossians is that only Christ is the head of all things in the church.** We are instructed in chapter 3:1-2, "seek those things which are above, where Christ sitteth on the right hand of God. Set your affection on things above, not on things of the earth."

(Colossians 2:6) "As ye have **therefore** received Christ Jesus the Lord, so walk ye in him;"

In chapter one, Paul speaks about how the gospel first came to the church at Colosse, and then offers a prayer for them which gives a description of Christ. Among those things said are that Christ is the head of the body (the church). Beginning the second chapter, Paul warns of any man beguiling them with enticing words and urges them to continue in Christ just the way they have received him. The result of this is pointed to in the next verse, the importance of keeping things exactly as they have been taught.

(Colossians 2:16) "Let no man **therefore** judge you in meat, or in drink, or in respect of an holyday, or of the new moon, or of the sabbath days:" This verse is a warning against rituals of the law which were abolished by the work of Christ. These things in the next verse are called a shadow of things to come. Christ was not the shadow, but the real thing, and his coming had replaced the shadow.

(Colossians 2:20) "**Wherefore** if ye be dead with Christ from the rudiments of the world, why, as though living in the world, are ye subject to ordinances," Verse twenty continues in the warning against those who would try to influence them by false "so-called" knowledge or philosophy. These things have a show of wisdom, will-worship, humility, and neglecting of the body.

(Colossians 3:5) "Mortify **therefore** your members which are upon the earth; fornication, uncleanness, inordinate affection, evil concupiscence, and covetousness, which is idolatry:" After the admonishing of chapter three, verse one: "If ye then be risen with Christ, seek those things which are above," they are told again in verse three, that being dead to the law, their life is with Christ. Therefore they are to put away the evil activities of this world. These are the things which cause the wrath of God. Christ is all in all.

(Colossians 3:12) "Put on **therefore**, as the elect of God, holy and beloved, bowels of mercies, kindness, humbleness of mind, meekness, longsuffering;" Having named and described the evil to be avoided, now Paul names the good which the elect of God are to do. This list includes not only the traits of mercy, kindness, humility, meekness, and longsuffering, but finishes with the instruction of their relationships to each other. These are forbearing, forgiving, and charity.

I THESSALONIANS: In his second recorded journey, after landing and spending time

in Philippi, Paul traveled south to Thessalonica. After a short time, he was chased on south by the enemies of his teaching. He had time to establish a church but was not able to stay long because of the persecution. This location was among the most immediate and violent persecutions of the early churches. Even by the time of his writing his very first epistle only a few months after leaving them, already many had been put to death. **The theme of this book is "hope."** In chapter 4, he encourages and comforts them concerning those who had already died in faith. "The dead in Christ shall rise first, then we which are alive and remain shall be caught up together with them in the clouds, to meet the Lord in the air: and so shall we ever be with the Lord." There is no greater strength for those in tribulation than the hope of the resurrection and Christ's victorious return to carry the church forward to its eternal home.

(I Thessalonians 2:18) "**Wherefore** we would have come unto you, even I Paul, once and again; but Satan hindered us." The church at Thessalonica is under great persecution which is described in the last part of chapter two. Paul himself was chased away from them under duress. He had received the report that they had held faithful to his teaching and is commending and comforting them. He wanted to come back to them but was not able.

(I Thessalonians 3:1) "**Wherefore** when we could no longer forbear, we thought it good to be left at Athens alone;" Paul was hindered from coming back to them himself, but had sent Timothy for the purpose of establishing and comforting them in their faith. The goal was that no man should be moved from their faith by these afflictions.

(I Thessalonians 3:7) "**Therefore**, brethren, we were comforted over you in all our affliction and distress by your faith:" Timothy had come from them to Paul with a good report and Paul is telling that it was a great comfort to him to receive this report. He urges them to continue.

(I Thessalonians 4:8) "He **therefore** that despiseth, despiseth not man, but God, who hath also given unto us his holy Spirit." Knowing that Christ is coming again, believers are warned about how they should walk while waiting. God has not called them to uncleanness, but unto holiness. The result of sanctification is something that is foreign to men, but those who hate men for it and persecute them are actually persecuting against God.

(I Thessalonians 4:18) "**Wherefore** comfort one another with these words." Prior to this verse, Paul has told them the order of things at the Lord's coming. The Lord himself shall descend from heaven with a shout with the voice of the archangel, and with the trump of God: and the dead in Christ shall rise first. Then those who are alive and remain shall be caught up together with them in the clouds, to meet the Lord in the air: and forever be with the Lord. Under persecution they are to comfort each other with these thoughts.

(I Thessalonians 5:6) "**Therefore** let us not sleep, as do others; but let us watch and be sober." Of course the believers wanted to know when this would happen. Paul says he is not to tell them of the time and season, but that they are to be watchful. They are not children of darkness and should not sleep, but they are to live in the light to see and understand and recognize as these things are about to come to pass. They are to put on the spiritual armour, the breastplate of faith and love; and for a helmet the hope of salvation.

(I Thessalonians 5:11) "**Wherefore** comfort yourselves together, and edify one another, even as also ye do." God has not appointed us to wrath but to obtain salvation. Christ died for us so that we would live together with him. So this verse is instruction for them in how to comfort and edify each other during this hard time. At the end of this chapter are actually twenty-two commandments for Christians to do.

II THESSALONIANS:
The church at Thessalonica had been remarkable in faithfulness under heavy persecution. They expected the Lord's immediate return. This letter written not long after the first one, was to reinforce their hope but tell them that it was not time yet. Certain things must come to pass, and they must be patient. **The theme of this epistle is patience to wait for the Lord's coming.** During their wait he encourages them to beware of false doctrines and teachings. These two epistles to a people in tribulation highlight how there are important spiritual blessings that accompany the foundation of faith. Two of those are hope and patience.

(II Thessalonians 1:11) "**Wherefore** also we pray always for you, that our God would count you worthy of this calling, and fulfil all the good pleasure of his goodness, and the work of faith with power:" In his first letter to the church at Thessalonica, Paul has told how the believers will be raised. Now he also tells in the previous verses of the judgement and destruction of the wicked. He tells that he prays for their obedient walk that they be counted worthy and that the name of Christ be glorified by them.

 (II Thessalonians 2:15) "**Therefore**, brethren, stand fast, and hold the traditions which ye have been taught, whether by word, or our epistle." Paul tells them of the evil that is present from Satan himself which will try to deceive them. But that God has chosen them to salvation from the beginning and will not lose them. To hold them in faithfulness is one of the purposes that he had called them by Paul's preaching the gospel to them. His last advice then is for them to be patient and stand fast and hold to the truths which they have been taught. The consolation given by Jesus Christ and God the Father is everlasting.

I TIMOTHY:
Paul first encounters Timothy in the city and church at Lystra, and Timothy accompanies Paul on his journey to Macedonia. Over the next fifteen years, until Paul's death,

Timothy is a constant traveling companion for Paul. Paul calls him "my own son in the faith." Timothy is named in eleven of the fourteen of Paul's epistles and also six times in the book of Acts. Paul gives Timothy both his instruction and his own example of being a faithful minister. He speaks to him about the qualifications of ministers, about their duties, about their commitment, and their behavior. Chapter 3:15 tells, "that thou mayest know how thou oughtest to behave thyself in the house of God, which is the church of the living God, the pillar and ground of the truth." **The theme of the book of 1st Timothy is the instruction and encouragement for pastors.** This is important for every church.

(I Timothy 2:1) "I exhort **therefore**, that, first of all, supplications, prayers, intercessions, and giving of thanks, be made for all men;" At the end of chapter one, Paul gives Timothy a charge, according to past prophecy, that he war a good warfare. A minister is for sure a soldier of the cross. Paul begins chapter two by describing public prayer and those things and people which Timothy should pray for.

(I Timothy 2:8) "I will **therefore** that men pray every where, lifting up holy hands, without wrath and doubting." Paul tells of his own calling as a preacher and apostle, appointed to preach the truth to the Gentiles in faith. He expresses here his desire to lead men into prayer and what their demeanor and position should be. He follows by also describing the same for women in the next two verses.

(I Timothy 4:10) "For **therefore** we both labour and suffer reproach, because we trust in the living God, who is the Saviour of all men, specially of those that believe." Paul has continued to give Timothy advice concerning the ministry. One thing to do is to teach truth when confronted with error. Another is to refuse profane and old wives' fables. He tells that physical exercise is of little profit, but that godliness is profitable and reinforces all these by saying "this is a faithful saying and worthy of all acceptation." Standing and preaching is going to cost something and be difficult work and will meet resistance. The next verse tells not to let men despise his youth, but to be an example of a believer.

(I Timothy 5:14) "I will **therefore** that the younger women marry, bear children, guide the house, give none occasion to the adversary to speak reproachfully." This verse is one of many in this chapter which give advice about the place of men and women and their duties and their place and what to expect. The previous verse is about some who spread gossip and dissention when they do not take a proper place of responsibility. More advice is given concerning supporting the widows and helpless and about teaching and the treatment of elders.

II TIMOTHY: The second epistle to Timothy was the farewell letter from Paul, and the last epistle which Paul wrote. Some of his prison letters were written from prison where he was well treated and simply under the watch of a guard. But now he was waiting his execution. His letter to Timothy was to encourage and admonish Timothy to continue the work and be strong. There will be persecution for all those who do this work right. He reminds him of his calling, he reminds him of the purposes of the scripture, he reminds him of the hardships. And then he admonishes him to be a good student of the scripture and a good soldier and endure hardness and to preach the Word. **The theme is to exhort Timothy and the saints in the ages to come to be faithful and endure hardness**

as a good soldier of Jesus Christ and continue the work of their spiritual calling. Older members have a responsibility to teach, model, and pass on the doctrines and practices of the church to the next generation, until the time when the Lord returns.

(II Timothy 1:6) "**Wherefore** I put thee in remembrance that thou stir up the gift of God, which is in thee by the putting on of my hands." The introduction of this letter to Timothy is an emotional one, a reminder of the blessings of God. He is reminded of his mother and grandmother and of how he was raised and how he had received a gift by the laying on of hands of Paul. There are great challenges ahead, but God did not give a spirit of fear, but of power and love and a sound mind.

(II Timothy 1:8) "Be not thou **therefore** ashamed of the testimony of our Lord, nor of me his prisoner: but be thou partaker of the afflictions of the gospel according to the power of God;" Christ had been crucified with the intent that believers would be made ashamed of him. Paul also as a prisoner to be put to death, was in that position in order to cause believers to be ashamed of him and his message. Paul instructs Timothy not to be ashamed either of him or his message. Further, their calling was from a God who had his own purpose before the world began and provided grace; and by what Christ had done, they had power over death. Death was what the enemy was threatening.

(II Timothy 2:1) "Thou **therefore**, my son, be strong in the grace that is in Christ Jesus." The second chapter begins with an expression which is meant to strengthen Timothy's position and resolve, as advice from a father to a son. He is Paul's son in the faith and in the ministry.

(II Timothy 2:3) "Thou **therefore** endure hardness, as a good soldier of Jesus Christ." There are many things to accomplish. First Timothy is to pass on his gift to other faithful men who will do the same work. Second, he is to realize that there is much hardship and that he must endure hardness as a good soldier of Jesus Christ. He must follow orders and fight the fight of the one who had called him to this spiritual work rather than getting entangled with natural affairs.

(II Timothy 2:10) "**Therefore** I endure all things for the elect's sakes, that they may also obtain the salvation which is in Christ Jesus with eternal glory." Paul continues by saying that he has been bound as a prisoner, but that the Word of God is not bound. So he endures being a prisoner so that the message of salvation can continue. Once more he calls it a faithful saying and that those who are dead with Christ will also live with Christ; those who suffer for him will reign with him.

(II Timothy 2:21) "If a man **therefore** purge himself from these, he shall be a vessel unto honour, sanctified, and meet for the master's use, and prepared unto every good work." In this chapter Paul has taught Timothy as a son, as an athlete, as a farmer, as a workman and teacher, and last of all as a vessel. He gives the example of a household with many vessels, some to honour and some to dishonour. Timothy is a vessel which has been cleansed by sanctification and is chosen and prepared for the Master's work.

(II Timothy 4:1) "I charge thee **therefore** before God, and the Lord Jesus Christ, who shall judge the quick and the dead at his appearing and his kingdom;" As Paul begins his last chapter to Timothy, he gives Timothy a charge. Paul himself is in a position of life and death. The subject of salvation is also one of life and death. The work that Timothy is to do is a matter of life and death. The first instruction which is a result of that seriousness, is that he preach the word in season an out of season. It was the work he was called to do and a matter of life and death.

TITUS: This epistle is the third of the "pastoral" epistles which not only instruct pastors, but also instruct churches about pastors and ministers. Titus is mentioned in four of the epistles and referred to in the book of Acts. Titus was a Gentile and was assigned ministry duty on the island of Crete. The instruction that Paul gives him and **the theme of this epistle to Titus concerns the requirements or conditions of a true church.** They are to be orderly, to be sound in doctrine, and to do good works. It is a duty of the ministry to see to these things.

(Titus 1:13) "This witness is true. **Wherefore** rebuke them sharply, that they may be sound in the faith;" The requirements of a church of God are not reached by accident or chance. By human nature, they would never happen. Paul is telling Titus that he must recognize the problems quickly and correct them firmly so that the church will be orderly and sound in doctrine. Chapter two continues that he is to speak those things which become sound doctrine.

PHILEMON:

The epistle to Philemon was one of the four epistles written during Paul's first imprisonment. This epistle and the one to Colosse were carried by the minister Tychicus and the slave Onesimus to the church at Colosse where Philemon was a member. Onesimus was an escaped slave of Philemon who had heard Paul preach and had become a Christian believer. Paul was returning him with this letter of recommendation to Philemon, his owner. **The theme here is Christian courtesy** and the lessons taught are forgiveness and the spiritual equality of God's people. The relationship between Onesimus and Philemon was now changed from master and slave to brothers in Christ.

(Philemon 1:8) "**Wherefore**, though I might be much bold in Christ to enjoin thee that which is convenient," The first verses of this book and chapter are a reminder of the bond of fellowship between Paul and Philemon, who is a member of the church at Colosse. Verse eight calls on that love between them for a favor that Paul will ask in the next verse. That he accept Onesimus, who Paul calls "his son." He further explains the situation to tell how Onesimus has become a believer and has been useful to Paul.

(Philemon 1:12) "Whom I have sent again: thou **therefore** receive him, that is, mine own bowels:" Here Paul is asking Philemon to accept Onesimus as though he were Paul himself. Paul tells that he first thought to keep Onesimus there but knew that wouldn't be right. So he was returning him to his owner, but now as a brother rather than a slave.

(Philemon 1:15) "For perhaps he **therefore** departed for a season, that thou shouldest receive him for ever;" Verse fifteen begins with this same thought, that now he is a brother. Maybe his running away was for the purpose of him becoming a believer and to arrive at a new relationship, both with God and with his master. The lesson here is symbolic of Christ's plea to the Father on behalf of the sinner for whom he has paid the price.

(Philemon 1:17) "If thou count me **therefore** a partner, receive him as myself." The guiltless substitutes himself for the guilty. Onesimus is received as if he is Paul. The sinner is received of God with the innocence of Christ. Paul pledges to pay any debt owed and expresses his confidence in Philemon to do the right thing.

HEBREWS:

While the writer of this book is not named, it is easy to assign it to Paul. The writer had been a prisoner in bonds (Hebrews 10:34), the epistle is written from Italy (Hebrews 13:24), the writer's companion was Timothy (Hebrews 13:23), and it is referred to by Peter, naming Paul as the writer (II Peter 3:15). This epistle is addressed to Christians of Jewish background and is a comparative study of the Jewish and Christian religions that show Christ is a better way. Better than Moses, better than the angels, better than the law, better than their sacrifices, and a better sanctuary. There is a special chapter in this book that stands out, showing the subject and importance of faith and those who had been faithful. Without faith it is impossible to please God. Jesus is shown as our high priest and now sits at the right hand of God as our intercessor. **The theme of this book is the priesthood of Christ and how it is "better."**

(Hebrews 1:9) "Thou hast loved righteousness, and hated iniquity; **therefore** God, even thy God, hath anointed thee with the oil of gladness above they fellows." Chapter one of this book shows the qualifications of Christ to be high priest. Among other things, he is shown to be better than the prophets, and then better than angels. The previous verses are about angels and how they worship the Christ. The eighth and ninth verses are quoting from the 45th Psalm. Christ is superior to angels because he rules over the entire universe, something the angels were never meant to do.

(Hebrews 2:1) "**Therefore** we ought to give the more earnest heed to the things which we have heard, lest at any time we should let them slip." If Christ is superior to the angels, the message of the last verses of chapter one, then we need to give heed to what we have heard and believe. The angels have told the truth of salvation and of Christ, and if everyone is rewarded for their transgressions, how would man ever escape if we neglect this salvation? Christ has authority over all.

(Hebrews 2:17) "**Wherefore** in all things it behoved him to be made like unto his brethren, that he might be a merciful and faithful high priest in things pertaining to God, to make reconciliation for the sins of the people." This section of chapter two points out that Christ became a man because the children of God were men. It was necessary that he overcome death in order to free men from the bondage and curse of death. The result is that he is now a comfort to men because he has gone through what they face.

(Hebrews 3:1) "**Wherefore**, holy brethren, partakers of the heavenly calling, consider the Apostle and High Priest of our profession, Christ Jesus;" The next step after showing he is superior to prophets and angels, is to show he is superior to Moses. Moses is the one who had brought the law from God. Moses had led them through the desert to the promised land and was the one that the Jewish religion was dependent on. Both Moses and Christ were faithful to their calling. But the house that Moses "built" was the tabernacle in the wilderness. The house of Christ is in the heavens and not measurable.

(Hebrews 3:7) "**Wherefore** (as the Holy Ghost saith, Today if ye will hear his voice," Moses was a faithful servant of God, but Christ was the Son of God. A son is better than a servant. Here is another quotation from the 95th Psalm. The point being made is that in each of the comparisons to Christ, the prophets and the angels and Moses all had spoken words. None were as important as the Word of God. God's own words include "my beloved son, hear ye him."

(Hebrews 3:10) "**Wherefore** I was grieved with that generation, and said, They do always err in their heart; and they have not known my ways." Starting with verse eight, it is speaking of the children of Israel coming out of Egypt. In the wilderness they did not believe and had to spend forty years there. The result was that an entire generation of those coming out of Egypt did not get to go in to the promised land because of their disbelief. That is a warning to God's children of all ages about the seriousness of disbelief.

(Hebrews 4:1) "Let us **therefore** fear, lest a promise being left us of entering into his rest, any of you should seem to come short of it." In chapter three and verse eleven, the promised land is called "my rest." Their disbelief prevented them from entering into it. It continues to describe that rest to the end of chapter three. Chapter four begins with the exhortation to do those things which would let us enter into that rest. The gospel of Christ is preached for the children of God to hear and believe.

(Hebrews 4:6) "Seeing **therefore** it remaineth that some must enter therein, and they to whom it was first preached entered not in because of unbelief;" Rest was likened here to the Sabbath which God gave for men to have rest every seventh day. God rested on the seventh day when his creative work was finished. Christ now rests, sitting at the right hand of God, now that his work of salvation has been completed. The works of man which God has ordained are the works which he does in the exercise of his faith because of his belief.

(Hebrews 4:9) "There remaineth **therefore** a rest to the people of God." This is referring to the book of Joshua. He led the people into the promised land and the taking and settling of it. But by the time of his old age and death that work was not complete. The people had not yet entered into all that was promised. The children of God today are the same. There awaits a heavenly rest for all of them.

(Hebrews 4:11) "Let us labour **therefore** to enter into that rest, lest any man fall after the same example of unbelief." God didn't rest on the seventh day because he was tired. He rested because his work was complete. Jesus is not resting at the right hand of God because he is tired, but because his work of salvation is finished. Man still has work to do here, his work is not finished. There is work for a believer to do. It is called worship, praising, exercising faith, and giving thanks.

(Hebrews 4:16) "Let us **therefore** come boldly unto the throne of grace, that we may obtain mercy, and find grace to help in time of need." The ending of chapter four highlights what a great and understanding high priest we have in Christ. The office and its purpose in the Old Testament was a practical one which was needed, depended on, and used by the people. The office today is also a practical one. By it we have one who knows our infirmities and temptations. His sacrifice was for a people who could then come boldly into his presence to find help in time of need.

(Hebrews 6:1) "**Therefore** leaving the principles of the doctrine of Christ, let us go on unto perfection; not laying again the foundation of repentance from dead works, and of faith toward God," There is a progression and spiritual growing that happens just like natural growing. The people of God are not supposed to get stuck on the first points of the foundation of their salvation and never reach maturity. Paul has mentioned in ending the last chapter how he has fed them with milk, as though they are infants. Perfection means completeness rather than being without any errors. And leaving the principles does not mean abandoning the basics of our beliefs. It means that there is more to salvation than the foundation, just like there is more to a house than its foundation. Without the foundation it would fall, but having a foundation, there is much more to the house which makes it useful and beautiful. This feature is pointed out by the use of a phrase referred to in verse nine, "those things which accompany salvation."

(Hebrews 7:11) "If **therefore** perfection were by the Levitical priesthood, (for under it the people received the law,) what further need was there that another priest should rise after the order of Melchisedec, and not be called after the order of Aaron?" There was a problem with the Aaronic priesthood. It was incomplete. It never brought perfection or redemption before God. It was necessary that there be a change in the order of priesthood, and Christ is that change.

(Hebrews 7:25) "**Wherefore** he is able also to save them to the uttermost that come unto God by him, seeing he ever liveth to make intercession for them." Throughout the years from the time of Aaron, there had been many high priests, because one by one they had all died. And the offerings for sin had to be repeated over and over again because they were imperfect and made by men who were sinners. Now there is one who is eternal that will never die, who is already seated beside the Father making intercession for his people. The old priests first had to make offerings for their own sins before entering in and offering for the people. Christ had no sin. His offering was perfect and only needed to be done once.

(Hebrews 8:3) "For every high priest is ordained to offer gifts and sacrifices: **wherefore** it is of necessity that this man have somewhat also to offer." The first verses of this chapter summarize what Israel had according to the law. However, what they had was a shadow of something to come. The first service of the shadow was set up by a covenant given unto the people in the days of Moses and Aaron. This is a new covenant, by a more excellent ministry, because Christ is the mediator of a better covenant which was established upon better promises.

(Hebrews 9:23) "It was **therefore** necessary that the patterns of things in the heavens should be purified with these; but the heavenly things themselves with better sacrifices than these." With the subject and answer being a "better" way, it was better in many ways. One of those was that there was a new sanctuary, better than the old one. The tabernacle on earth was simply a type of the heavenly one to come. The earthly one is described in the previous verses. And in the next verse it clarifies further that Christ is not entered into the holy places made with hands, but into heaven itself and into the presence of God.

(Hebrews 10:5) "**Wherefore** when he cometh into the world, he saith, Sacrifice and offering thou wouldest not, but a body hast thou prepared me:" The service of the law was only a shadow of good things to come. Those things being offered had to be done over and over because they didn't fulfill the requirements. They were not perfect and didn't fulfill the prophecies of what was to come. The bodies of animals were not acceptable to God, except as a type and shadow of what was to come. But God himself prepared a sacrifice and a perfect offering in the body of his son.

(Hebrews 10:19) "Having **therefore**, brethren, boldness to enter into the holiest by the blood of Jesus," God had promised in the days of Jeremiah, that he would put a new covenant and laws in the hearts and minds of his people, and that by it the sins and iniquities would be forgotten. With the remission of these sins, no more offering is required. Now rather than by the death of a sacrifice, we may enter into the presence of God in a new and living way which was accomplished by the blood of Christ. Reference is made in verse twenty-two of the sprinkling of the blood of the sin offering, "having our hearts sprinkled from an evil conscience and our bodies washed with pure water." And the result of these should be devout worship, encouraging one another.

(Hebrews 10:35) "Cast not away **therefore** your confidence, which hath great recompence of reward." Paul reminds these believers of the persecutions they have had for believing the truth. He is urging them to stand faithful and not fall back in the face of danger.

(Hebrews 11:12) "**Therefore** sprang there even of one, and him as good as dead, so many as the stars of the sky in multitude, and as the sand which is by the sea shore innumerable." Chapter eleven is the chapter on faith and of those who exercised it. The previous verse speaks of Sara and her conception at an old age of the child of promise which would have descendants on the earth that are uncountable. Even though Sara and Abraham had the son, they didn't live long enough to see their offspring inherit the land of promise. But by faith they believed in it.

(Hebrews 11:16) "But now they desire a better country, that is, an heavenly: **wherefore** God is not ashamed to be called their God: for he hath prepared for them a city." These who had died in faith not having received the promises, confessed that they were strangers and pilgrims on earth. They were waiting and longing for a heavenly country, an even greater land than the one promised them here on earth.

(Hebrews 12:1) "**Wherefore** seeing we also are compassed about with so great a cloud of witnesses, let us lay aside every weight, and the sin which doth so easily beset us, and let us run with patience the race that is set before us," Having told of so many who were faithful, each generation of God's people have also been surrounded by those with faith and hope. The duty of those who have received such a hope is that we lay aside the requirements of the law and follow the instructions and rejoicing of grace on the path of the life given to us. Just like it gave great joy to Christ to do that in his path, it is possible for his people to also joy in it if they keep their eyes on him.

(Hebrews 12:12) "**Wherefore** lift up the hands which hang down, and the feeble knees;" It is promised that there will be tribulation in this life on earth. Because of sin and human nature, the path of life is never easy. But it is much easier if believers are encouraging and helpful to each other. It is easier to walk with those who believe and those who pray for each other, than to walk alone. There is more honor in bearing a cross faithfully or helping another with his burden, than in living a life of easiness. The goal is faithfulness not easiness.

(Hebrews 12:28) "**Wherefore** we receiving a kingdom which cannot be moved, let us have grace, whereby we may serve God acceptably with reverence and godly fear:" The previous two verses mention the voice which spoke and shook the heavens and the earth. God is the one of all power and purpose and his purposes will be complete and victorious. Through the ages, men and kingdoms have fought against God and his people. But those have fallen one at a time through all the ages. Sometimes it may seem that good and God are losing and that evil is winning. But it is only temporary, God's kingdom is one that cannot be moved, changed, or defeated. Knowing this leads God's people in a faithful way to serve him acceptably.

(Hebrews 13:12) "**Wherefore** Jesus also, that he might sanctify the people with his own blood, suffered without the gate." There was an altar of worship and sacrifice under the law and there is one in heaven now. The blood of fifteen hundred years of sacrificing animals on that altar of the law did not change the nature of man. But the sacrifice and the blood of Christ has accomplished it at the altar in heaven. Jesus was crucified outside the city because he was a sin offering for his people. The sin offering was taken away from the temple and the law.

(Hebrews 13:13) "Let us go forth **therefore** unto him without the camp, bearing his reproach." So now Paul is telling the Hebrews who became Christian believers that it is ok to leave the temple and the law service. Paul knew that becoming a believer would draw scorn and reproach and persecution. He had done it and he had been persecuted. Christ died that those sacrifices didn't need to be made any more and believers were no more in bondage to the law. They were free from it now.

(Hebrews 13:15) "By him **therefore** let us offer the sacrifice of praise to God continually, that is, the fruit of our lips giving thanks to his name." The last "therefore" in Paul's writing is a fitting final exhortation to the believer. These things all being true concerning Christ as our perfect high priest, command us to live and be a certain way. Our voices should be raised in songs of praise and the very utterings of our souls be prayers of devotion until our change come.

CONCLUSION: The epistles were written for the use of the church, for the foundation of its doctrine, practice, and order. Besides the fourteen epistles studied here, the seven epistles of James, Peter, John, and Jude have the same purpose, each having a theme and exhortations for God's people to follow. It is important to remember that the church is not "man's" but God's. It is a spiritual body referred to as the bride of Christ and church triumphant, as well as a physical body referred to as the church militant. Christian believers are given the responsibility to care for it, to use it as it was intended, and to keep it as it was given. Every point of truth in the Bible leads to a result and conclusion that is good for the child of God and good for the church.

Printed in Dunstable, United Kingdom